JED PASCOE'S
THE FUNNY SIDE OF 40

FOR HIM

First Published in Great Britain by
Powerfresh Limited
3 Gray Street
Northampton
England
NN1 3QQ

Telephone 0604 30996 Country Code 44
Facsimile 0604 21013

© January 1993 Jed Pascoe

THE FUNNY SIDE OF 40 FOR HIM
ISBN 1 874125 10 4

Printed in Britain by Avalon Print Ltd., Northampton.

OH, RIGHT! SO THAT'S WHAT A TON-UP BOY WAS!

HEY, DAD! COME AND SHOW US HOW YOU BECAME WORLD SKATEBOARDING CHAMPION IN 1968...

WHO SAYS ROMANCE IS DEAD AT OUR AGE?...!

I JUST THINK THAT YOU SHOULD CONSIDER A LITTLE
TRAINING BEFORE YOU PLUNGE INTO A SECOND CAREER..

I'M NOT SAYING HE'S OLD. BUT HIS IDEA OF A RISING MEGA-STAR IS CHARLIE CHAPLIN!

FOR THIRTEEN YEARS, WE HAVEN'T BEEN ABLE TO GET HIM WITHIN TWENTY-FIVE FEET OF A SHOWER...

BUT NOW HE'S DISCOVERED GIRLS, ALL THE RUDDY HOT WATER'S GONE!

DAD, I'M NOT GOING OUT WITH YOU DRESSED LIKE <u>THAT</u>!

HOW CAN YOU SHRINK FOOTBALL BOOTS... ?

WHEN, EXACTLY, <u>WAS</u> THE LAST TIME YOU FLEW IN AN AIRCRAFT, SIR?

DON'T WORRY, MUM...
GEOFFREY'S GOT AN
'O' LEVEL FOR WOODWORK...
HAVEN'T YOU, GEOFFREY?

DAD'S SKATING GETS 10 OUT OF 10 FOR EFFORT, BUT ZERO FOR STYLE..

SUPPORT FALLEN BELOW AVERAGE THIS YEAR, VICAR?

TOO OLD TO BE A TOY-BOY, TOO YOUNG TO BE A
SUGAR-DADDY... LIFE'S TOUGH WHEN YOU'RE HIS AGE..

MM - YOU HAVEN'T WORN THAT SUIT FOR A WHILE...

MARK MY WORDS, SIR, YOU WILL SOON GROW INTO THEM

SOUNDS LIKE IT'S TIME TO BUY A NEW DINNER SUIT....

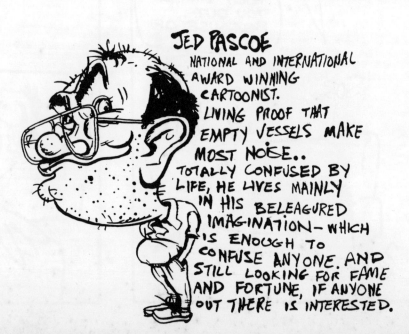

JED PASCOE
NATIONAL AND INTERNATIONAL AWARD WINNING CARTOONIST.
LIVING PROOF THAT EMPTY VESSELS MAKE MOST NOISE..
TOTALLY CONFUSED BY LIFE, HE LIVES MAINLY IN HIS BELEAGURED IMAGINATION — WHICH IS ENOUGH TO CONFUSE ANYONE. AND STILL LOOKING FOR FAME AND FORTUNE, IF ANYONE OUT THERE IS INTERESTED.